As Time Goes By

A Collection of Poetry and Prose

Kollin Kennedy

Contents

To Reader,

Before you embark on the journey of reading my work, I wish to provide some argument and explanation to prevent any confusion or misunderstanding of these poems I would for your satisfaction. These poems are merely as miniatures one would see on coins or within the necklace: an art giving pleasure without having so gargantuous a canvas. I've written other poem portraits before of greater length, but the sonnet format continues to captivate my fancy as one of the greatest forms Calliope hast gifted us versers. However, I believe the sonnet has much more to offer readers other than depicting the poet's discontent of the world, and it's through this collection I've experimented mine mightier sword. The collections come from inspirations I found amusing in books, film, song, painting, or other accounts of humanities. I care not to relate a story connecting the sonnets to an underlying meaning, as in previous self-published collections I did so and failed miserably in its terrible complexity, nor care if the verse uses language of ancient times or coins words that seem not to fit with modern creativity. For mine only intention is to write with truth and honesty, as well as with experiments of poetic forms and unmodern syntax, while being clear as the verse permits. I wish not to measure the beats out of the bounds of conception, but would to put myself in the heads of other characters of art that, as I think, have much more beauty in the soul of their tongues than the prose that depicts them. If it revives archaic and ancient wording or uses forms of measures so unknown to our state of art, I only hope to inspire enjoyment and please the reader. If this is not your idea of modern poetry, please leave this book; for I've no use for thee if you're uptight about 'thy' 'thou' or 'methinks', or if the subjects are offensive to the Mickey-mouse eye. These works are as Montaigne essays, collections ranging of different topic as I feel them, though I myself am not the sole matter of this book, and I've no time for petty matters. If you like these works, I'm grateful to you; if not, I've no reason to force your eyes to my measures and I only hope I win your affection back next time.

As you read, you may wonder why the titles of some sonnets have more wording than needs be. If you see First Perspective in the title, it means I'm writing in the first person perspective as I conceive that certain character, inspired of book, film, or painting, were to communicate if he or she had the hand on the written verse. Conceive of it as you would read either in first person perspective for a fantasy or literary fiction, or in the likes of a Caravaggio, Rembrandt, or Velazquez depicting many faces that are different from their own though communicating the soul of the differing creature. If you see Study in the title, it means I wrote the poem as a work intended to help me with a greater or larger project, in the likes of the thousandth Michaelangelo study to better practice him of the final Sistine Chapel. Some poems include both. The few that have A Study on the Humors are the sonnets intended for comedic experiments only, trying to figure out what words, philosophies, ironies, or errors within writing that make people laugh; the word 'humors' as I intended it has no relation to the four humors of humorism.

The satirical letters follow the same format as the poems, as I put myself in characters, part inspired by life as well as book, and write as their perspective as I think they would if they were doubting or criticizing a certain area of art they find distasteful or not too pleasant in a much exaggerated and absurd way with a letter format; but at the end of they day, purported to speak out honest in the vain of humor. These letters were more for fun than serious art, without much significance to the titles; but, as with the poems, built for the entertainment and pleasure for the reader.

Now that I've given my argument, it is up to you, dear reader, to take my words for what they mean, and I hope it may inspire your soul to at least one-half the rapture of my soul when writing them. I thank you for taking the time of your hours to entertain yourself with my verse and prose.

K. Kennedy

The Poems

The Seascape

Traumatic sheets cover Neptune's army
In their navy sleep, tossing & turning
Them with fancies of the next salty war
They must pointlessly face, directed by
Some looney archer whose virgin for war
Is far away of the present age.
Those blue soldiers fail at any rest
And will attack all opposite earth
That comes a threat —for I've eyed a scene
Where a sailor sailed on their theater,
Thiefed his compass, drowned his mates, & lost him
Of his island to find another
And held him captive for seven twelve-months.
They're blue, & their youthful anger comes of
Sadness; when they coast & on their guard,
They prepare for waves of violent blueness.

The Egyptian Girl

From mine measures, thou art receives no verse
To equal thy Cleopatrean curse
Of beauty, & I'm left to vulgar shapes
To picture you: thy bronze torso & hips
Clean as the purest white, thy mouth a red rose
Open for birds & bees; thy little nose,
Breast, & visage seduce to thy hymen
That gives airs of marriage to all men.
Thou art's a crown of observation
And arouses mine deadly cupid's passion;
For this, I would to insert this staff of love
To you to receive me, as Daphne's dove
Within that forest, for us to be as one
And be the image of love under the sun.

'Tis Dangerous

'Tis dangerous of we to keep this affair
Within the tummelment of jealous airs
Our artificial world so lively breathes.
Our love's too human, too with the leaves
That're too with greenness by Big Brother's eyes;
But it's through thee, within our truthful lies,
I find conclusion to my tales, mine spirit
Penetrating thy soul, with my heart sent
To Cytherea's top within thy love.
I check no items, nor do I ask above
For graven vanities; all I hope
'S that within this earth our love may cope,
As the world 'comes less human by the age
And makes true love to be found by the stage.

Though you speak of Love as a blindèd child
With one who staffs of love made them defiled
And seem to want love without passionments,
Methinks your play on love lacks measurements
To the verse & knows not the affection
One comes away with under Love's fashion
When embraced by divine embraces
Of a lusty nature, or when faces
Mouth loving O's on the wood of Love's stage.
All love has had an underperformed page,
But this is no reason to flip it off
And judge its cover; allow you to loft
And make up with love as I'll with you,
As only this will bond you to a love true.

You Made Me Love You

I know not thou art or thy motive
To love me, if it's by your will to live
Or to ring my bell's end to fool around
Then fall for the next Adam. The mound
For reason, I could careless of its heart
As you made me love you by that lost art
So few women have: charm, elegance
Without pomp, flirt & feminine sense,
Despite thy visage ere Mona Lisa.
Some have work done or brag of their visa
And for this I'm at shy for modern love;
But you're nat'ral, using what God above
Gave you in gifts of grace for thy beauty
To make me want all thy love I see.

Study of an Athlete, First-Person Perspective

Ere vulgar opinion, I'm once a man
Training me to overcome mine Adam's state
To meet a Michelangelo image
Or other any visage of the clouds;
For I'm mine own hand, will, & reason
As man's the center of his own art,
Taking discipline as life & death
For my sport's pleasure, so those in the stands
Who eat unstale breads to our world's circus
Enjoy the manly indulgence I give.
Criticizement & other pokey holes
Are mere child's play, as I'm no ear to them;
For I'm an athlete & for mine own sport
To take mine passions for love on the court.

The Study of an Athlete in the Vain of The Greek

Of rigorous art & Samsonesque arm
Our athlete of vigor stands, with proportions
Zeus-like to his mountains of bicep,
Triceped valleys, vicious strings of his leg,
Bat-winged latissimus, & temple to
Connect the torso fine to reason's home
That may conceit one to myth for his strength
To feat off Nemean lions or other
Distressful labors. Unsteroided
And nat'ral, our athlete's worthy of
Vitruvius in his architecture
Of perfect numbers & art's alabaster,
As no other accomplish could be man
Unless a divine worked him of his right hand.
A poet of poems, an American, hast left this verse…

Cupio Dissolvi, in the Vain of Saint Paul

Mine heart's perplexed & contains mystery
In a duel of doubt: my life's for heaven,
Though to live under I am Flesh's dust,
With each mortal spec sin to creation,
Though this is mine labor's fruit. To die's to gain
And with Him to live is far the better
Than the sufferance of earth's debacle:
To dissolve, to depart is what I sing
And would upon mine image. But again,
Abiding by the flesh is Heaven's law
And needful of our world's purpose for good;
In this light, I shall have furtherance,
Keeping my works in pleasure to The One
So my returns to Him are above the sun.

The Portrait of A Nice Guy, First Perspective

I do unto others as unto me:
Relate respect, have class, make two a three;
With love, I kiss the hand before the lips
And make mine measures no measure for hips
As I would to respect the lady's quest
For this advancement. I treat all the best,
But I'm the doormat to all open doors
When I'm this: most dust me off to the floors
Making me flesh, while women reject the nice
Taking me too virtuous for the vice
Of love. All in all, I'm a sweet nothing
Without any to take me for something,
And within me there's a disgust for this
As the niceness brings me not any bliss.

The Playboy, A Study

Your love is without measure as I give
You mine, & permits my freedom to live
Outside our love for another measure,
To come away of another pleasure.
Your lack of measures may come off disgraced
To some, taking love's value by the face,
But I careless of these starch puritans,
As I live modernly to all my sins;
In fact, to those under Hymen's measures
Seem not for their other rib to treasure,
And are but with them to not be alone.
I live to the triumph of mine own Rome!
So I praise you for your lack of measures
As I'm man away of wifely pressures.

The Hopeless Romantic, Under the Vain of Great Gatsby

My love is out there, by the Venus light,
Though Nature's law forbids me of her sight
Only my mind's eye can see. I go out
And converse the weather without a doubt
To each ladybug who lay on poppies,
But each lick leads not my bird to these bees,
Flying me back to my nest egg of woe
In the yolk of wonderance if I'll know
The truth of my love. Of course there are lies
And one must sleep on them as he tries
His love; but as the world becomes more earth
Lies in love becomes the truth to his mirth,
With this to leave me confused as a dove
And in waits to know what awaits my love.

The Portrait of Sisyphus, First Perspective; A Study

Within my past life, I oppressed for fun
All creeping things equal under the sun;
But now, by some unlucky Fortune of the wheel,
The gods have fated me to no appeal
For higher heavens, leaving me to
The uncultured law of vile Hades' hue.
Mine punishment 's rolling up a rock
To down it again, molested in walk
With the mononature of existence
That lacks art, beauty, & the truth of sense.
I rue the day of mine begetment!
I was wise & thought I was heaven sent,
But I cannot forelay my past a new:
'Tis stuck in stone, & life gives not chances two.

Beyond the Sea, from a 20th Century Sailor

Somewhere, beyond these wakes of Neptune;
Beyond this lowly vessel I find me
In, assuming stance, my other half
Patients for me to return my service
And meet her my Cupid to her Venus
In the beloads of our humble abode.
Sometimes, I would to jump ship of duties
And escape to love's enduring bosom;
However, the feat would disrespect me
Of practice & would lose mine art of love
For the girl who envisions my virtue.
Though this world's flat with mythie loneliness,
I'll keep my love's image to my mind's eye
And sleep with it if by these waters I die.

Dedication to Velazquez

Whose art surpasses that of art itself,
Who captures the all of Spain's glory himself
I dedicate this wounded verse to thee
To endure thy praise in a work from me
Inspired of thy painting beyond genius,
Beyond divinity you gave to Venus,
That imaged the Immaculate Virgin
With the Trinity in fleshly person.
O Beauty! O Art! O Virgin Mary!
Thou art painted delights over-merry
In vigor of the simple, as Mozart's
Pieces of finesse with form in the parts;
And with these measures, hope I all mortals see
The greatness you put to earth I try to be.

Self-Portrait

With endurement to life's enduring storms
Though relief comes not at Nature's request,
Methinks I hold life to a prejudice
And oft bring mine own sufferment from mine
Own doing. Sure, there's bad babes from good wombs
To inspire war & famine, pox that beget
From doubts, & other mysteries that our dogs
Can but dictate; but as a man of man,
I have choosing whether mine heart's free
Or succumb to pangs of a woeful chest
By the health of reason. I can take life
By her nature, or believe her fickle;
Either way, I'm the center of my soul
And the one only to make it whole.

Thou art quivers Cupid's arrows nicely:
With passion; but with thy target in place,
Come away without thy aim precisely
To mine heart. For I would to keep my case
Without the cytherean mystery
Lurking my bosom. I've been bemuddled,
Taken to hoodwinks, amoked, led astray,
And flat out deceived, blindly befuddled,
From those unconscious pricks by Love staffs
That engage me to mine lover's folly.
Even if you have visage or make laughs,
Commit thy attacks for a slow dally;
But alas! I've no control over thee
And but admit to flames you insight to me.

A Long Love

Mine love is long, &'ll keep up with thee
As long as the clock hast time with me,
With thou art ready of a love long.
Many a lover's love is short & wrong:
But able to stay up to come away
Once the passion dies, without taking stay
On the love to revive it better
And come with love when the love's together.
There's no length, no width, no height in most love,
With most resorting to some soul above
In dreams to relive this affection;
But if thou art trust mine loving fashion,
Take mine long love, & stomach it with me
And let not an inch escape for one to see.

We'll Meet Again

We'll meet again, in spite thou art gone,
With our souls transmigrated to games on thrones,
By a tower, a station, where kids greet,
Or another earth where heavens meet.
This world suffers by nature, making tears
A custom canny to life's selfsame fears;
The faults within our space 's regular
And we must pursue our course the better
Regardless of the human condition
Plaguing us doubts in our premonition.
Collect thy sorrows & keep a face;
We'll meet once more, within of God's grace,
As methinks there's a world over yonder
That means our lives in spirits to wonder.

Inspired of Michelangelo

Father above, release me of myself
In mine conduct, degrees, tones, & vile force
I own to verses, that conceits to chump change,
And 'spire my writes so I may please Thou Art
In my measures. Mine couplets are centered
And selfish, echoing moans of flowers
Just to eye the own pretty reflection,
Without touching man's heart & mystery
And giving the posy its endurance.
I admit my marks & show my mincemeat
In its tender & rotten fashioned flesh,
And its but with Thy mighty right hand
I can forget this weakness & glorify
Before Thy name, ere mine words are to die.

The Trial of Despair

I know not the long mine mortal mettle
Has juice to keep its flame, or if my years
Has enough age to live me through life's game:
For Nature's grimmy looks show too much its face
And every day Despair makes brows of woe
To compliment the visage; I meekly work,
But methinks mine inheritance is none;
Friends are few, & Cupid's extinct for me,
And my only slight of satisfaction
Is waking up to mine lost unconscious
Or imitate Niobe in my alas.
This life is a stock to our world's stage,
With all men pitying this tragedy
Without helping mine act out its mockery.

I mind not thy lies with various men
Who confess their lies as love before sin:
For you lie to them to protect virtue
Of some kind, so they won't further pursue
Their lies on love. But when thou art eyes me
And regards my lies, thy love nighs me,
As you act as you've never lied with one
For love & allowed thou lies for none.
Thou art's a liar & you've proven such
With the intent of love behind your much,
But there's no need to act a fool for love
When all of our lies are seen from above;
So as we both lie & love together,
Let us make our love from lies for the better.

If I May Find A Fortress of Solitude...

I wish to retreat me of all things
And make my days the seventh day for rest;
My labors are lost of love, & people
Are more like creeping things than humanist:
Making gods of themselves though believe none,
Crawl on dead presidents, infect themselves
With virus, & chase the wind like a game
Of spades to take in life's many tricks
Without solve to any. Within retreat,
I'll resort to nature & find beauty
Within her, 'stead of superficial broads
Over weak vessels, so I may find peace
Beyond my flesh that sense attachments
On this earth that are shallow as they're sent.

Thy cherub-like face of innocence,
Pupils where live Oceanus seas,
Thy mind without knowing or without sense
That has sentenced sin on many Eves,
With thy smooth & chilted skin better
Than an art's alabaster; & lips full
Of Venus that verse poetic measure,
Limbs as grapevines that seduce the Taurus bull
Of his love's stubbornness, & thy complete
Figure out-graces the Graces for youth
Become you will the fourth grace. You're a treat
For any verser to know Beauty's truth,
And I end these delights for all age
So the world may enjoy thee by this page.

A Sonnet For An Old Lover

I've come away of thy love for another.
Act not surprised of this feat, or bother
Me contentious to live on a housetop,
As you've pushed me to with our mateship.
Done I am taking the heart of a fool
Just for thy love that you would to tool
In seeming affection; I'm mutt to thee
Following your path that disrespects me
In each eye of man. With my new love
I'm treated as a man came from above:
She is Eve & takes me for Adam,
And I've no time for thy vile sodom;
So measure me if you wish, I care not,
As I look on you as that wife of Lot.

When flirting you to me of thy venus love,
Thy tongue's ambiguous of measure
And speaks in gray area of thy want
In affection, leaving me confounded
To discover thy mystery of heart.
I'm no brain translator, or Casanova
With tricks of trade to unpuzzle thy piece
Of missing desire; you must tell me you,
The soul of your want, to miss these child games
For me to go down on thy peach of love
And leave thy fruit open for more desserts.
With no answers, you leave thy fruit dry,
With me waiting for you to use thy speech
So I may engage me to thy best beseech.

Stars cross to thwart love, the oceans crash
Sailors from their Ithaca, a vile rash
Cherries the flesh; the gods can be jealous
And lie with thy lover, seeming careless,
While Fortune can ease a stringy fate
And conceit all Venus on me to hate.
Without thy love, the universe is none:
The moon is merely moon, the sun is sun,
These Nature's gifts compare not to thee
As they shine on mine loneliness to see.
Yes, Nature's a true impressionist;
But her impression on me made a bad first,
As she's made all of earth a musty mess
If one has no love to comfort his bliss.

On Alcestis

Our ancestor's pagan Mary thou art,
Who offered Death the manners of thy heart,
Has exalted virtue beyond bodies
Of the weakest vessel, as our Lord sees
For men, in your sacrifice to let thy
Admentus, thy virtuous husband, lie
Safe of life, & offspring well under birth.
Though thy fam will praise Saturn for mirth,
Letting sorrow reign, & thou husband's art
Will doubt in cowardism in his heart
For his unsacrifice, thy soul will live on
As example for ladies who are pawn
In life, who carry mettle for themselves
And no pomp for children for their own health.

Where Did Our Love Go?

Once, we fooled around as War & Love
With but the fears below & that above
Smithing us for our further affair;
We cared no regret, nor what's foul or fair,
And came away with mirth by each union.
But now, my soul 's never near thy person
And I'm let to confusement of our Love.
Wherefore did our Love go? Did a Jove
Find us out? Was our Love given chastise?
Or did the gold lead us on its loving size?
Whatever the doubt, I'm confounded
And mad at the surprise, as it sounded
As our Love would endure to array
As long as the world had the eye of day.

'Tis Pity She's A Whore

Though the verse I've laid I've measured before,
But 'tis a pity the woman's a whore
Who exploits herself out her own asset,
Letting exploits come to her lostèd wit.
Though by each second she'll get her quarters
And live Independence by our fathers,
She knows not, methinks, as her products moist
They decay by age & its value from choice
Of many customers; but her business
Partners indulge her & voice to her bliss
Sweet nothings that keep her for the streets.
Soon, she'll meet where all Jezebel meet
As Ahabs advantage her, though many
Would not to offend her horns of plenty.

Confession I

Though my mortal statue looks virtuous,
Presenting pomps & crowning airs for goodness
To my duties, methinks a spirit lies
Under me unmanly, as my soul flies
As a lion, the animal of the sun,
That took in lesser natures for his tongue
And feels now the effects of his consumption.
I've studied with a manly canon,
But my nerves make contrary my true heart
With doubts in mine virtuous part
If mine offerings are worthy of heaven
Or if this image I create is for sin;
I'm filled with suspicion, but I pray
Mine work's worthy ere mine heart's to lay.

On The Dignity of Man

Man, God's most liberal invention, has wills
Made in His image, to dethrone the brute
In him & crown to a nature higher
Among the Seraphim & Cherub spheres;
For his art for reason, skill for self-law,
And soul to coin portraits from his mind's eye
Sets him from the things that creep on this earth.
But with these gifts, one must pursue knowing
The renewal of his mind, either through book,
Gospel, and or in treatments with mankind,
So his presence won't be a praise for folly
But may glorify the heavens' name,
With all a face made fresh by his tributes
To our world, that will endure as strife rebutes.

Confession II

I am not what I am: I have a heart
Made of dust, veins that are a kin to flesh,
Unmighty right hands that share as my left,
And a spirit, though longing for heavens,
That can warp for Hades if I try for
Omniscience, like that fallen angel
That once brought light. You may think me as a sprite
For tales, or something but poets can coin,
But I am man, maybe even lower,
And hold bosoms that's of our earth's begat,
And wish not to cherub as a Seraphim
For I've much to learn ere I'm divine
Which takes epochs to our measly world's age
And more of what is written yond this page.

Humanism

With life, one must suffer for his chances
To be on the button with Fortune
As her nature's wheel arounds with blindness,
And's quick to fail us ere we succeed
And stay fickle to thief us of our hopes,
As we cry operas that's made for soaps.
But though they're sufferments before our wins,
A slothy soul is the worst of all sins,
And it's better if we fought for our right,
Than give up & doubt on the soul of might,
To overcome nature & be human.
Our divine pow'r is to all under the sun
And we can become more than our being
As our sights are small to what we're seeing.

The Portrait of Thérèse Raquin, First Perspective

Mine visage has been purest Mary
Obeying my house, as a fairy
Without much tinker to her limbs, as long
As mine mortal memory stands along;
Though I've acquired bliss from this taking,
Methinks of my life I've lived in faking.
For violence that lust my soul from heaven
Would not to see wholeness, but would to sin
And reap excesses poet's keep in verse
From nature, & be hit by Cupid's curse
In love, to rebel my upbringing
That was chorused in song for angels singing,
And this husband who's limp as he is shaved
From desire, so with love I may be saved.

The Portrait of Admiral Ackbar, Before the Battle of Endor; First Perspective

Our profits are slim to this war exchange
That plagues our galaxies for spacely change
From the groted Imperial Force we fight,
But we must persist our sabers in might
While our going is marred & lasers mark
Our every sight. No wins come from yelling hark
And taking each sound as a double duchess
Jumping to feet, though naive to bliss
In thinking the battles will end on their own
Without her influence. For you're not alone
As it takes a fleet to wipe an empire,
And our rebels will be as men till our tire
To bring balance to the force in all earths
And a just peace from unjustly war mirths.

The Portrait of Billy Rae; or The Son of a Preacher, First Perspective

Though mine heart's design is within my fam
In puring ourselves equal to the lamb,
My youth strikes me as lecherous, & sinned
With penny heads for dime pieces. Offend
Not in my game: I put on face for smoothness
To please all from my lies to help their bliss;
But when darkness is empty & I can
Heckle ways to truth, I become a Pan
And come away dead to each Venus child.
Mine father's law concocts shadows mild
Within me from deprivement of nat'ral reigns,
And nothing is to suit for it but pangs
That erupts from some musty minion from Hell
And follies stories in me from earth's tales.

Self-Portrait, On Images

Every chaste call that mine mortal compass
Inherits from heavens, in taking alas
Virtuous with mirth, disporting myself
Without weaker vessels, & tailing my health
To that of gentle & cogent fibers,
There's rebel in me of maran livers
That would to gall over earth's seductments
And beck an Epicurus contentment
To ease the mortifiment of my soul
And happy as a part in not as whole.
For I wish the sun to halo my head,
But methinks more when I'm dreaming in bed
And conceit pictures that divide my image
That God has coined for man in His visage.

Vulgar Sonnet I

Quit this tartuffe of virtue, & love me
As those lovers you once held above me;
For I know thou art & thy history
That thou would jail of mortal memory,
And know thy nature is deadly with lust
That leaves thy other sins within your trust
Of control, though thou would to deceive me
With signals that doubt not to conceive me
Of some sex. The many clasp hands you make
And the love that you've given from your take
Confuse not the heavens from your Hades;
And as man the same love is for ladies,
So shadow not thy affections for more
Or I'll come away for another whore.

The Portrait of Sheev Palpatine, A Study; First Perspective

Pow'r is none 'less pow'r overs omniscience
Presiding with good & evil for control,
And methinks I'm a miser to one
And possess change of the other, when mine like
Desires forceful wreaths of both. I train for good
And please mine deadly sins, but it's nothing
To what methinks the Force can arm in an heart;
And this vile pest that Nature puts to man
Disrupts my soul's sun from any summers
And leaves a thunderous cloud to woo me.
I'm in pieces, yet I would them for whole
As balance in our forces is man's goal,
But I must be an angel to the dust
As man pleases me not in our world's rust.

Beauty & Ugliness

Believe you that ugliness all tells lies
While beauty tells truth, & when Love flies
You leave the foul & are quick to the fair
Without thought like an arrogant hare
Racing a tortoise. However, your sense
Is blinded in Love's glitter over small pence
As sometimes beauty lies to the beholder
And deceives meaning over one's shoulder;
So this one you consider all truthful
For his fresh airs & his loving youthful
May give you sweet lies for your pretty days
Ere he confesses truth & comes away
Of you, while I give you no lie but truth
In mine ugliness to reprieve you of ruth.

In The Name Of Love

Hit I've been by more arrows I would stand
In the realm of Love, though I'm no command
To the coming bows out his lusty quiver
But would to end his constant love's summer
That makes me constant in heat. All visage
Is a Daphne, though I chase the image
Of Xanthippe, when I'm struck by Love
And each smile is something Beatrice above;
I can't take this youth as I waste time
And but chase trees by the end of his crime!
I call out to him to halt his madness
So I may return to The One with bliss,
As all this fooling around is child's play
And won't mettle my soul by the end day.

The Mysterious Blonde

With mine Cupid's eye, I found mine true love;
Though her visage's unclear, from above
Methinks this cytherean came away
To confess me her passions! Today
She came as a fast fancy, but drove off
With her weary image for me to love off
The negative. All mine know's that she's blonde
And wants mine soul & hers for love to bond.
Find I must this fourth grace! The other three
That conceit looks have not grace enough for me,
Nor any other walking Eve of earth.
I must find this one! Eve' if it takes my mirth,
As I know she'll be the savior of bliss
And unlock me of dreadful loneliness.

We Must Part

Though our enchantments are as laughing Love
In the mood for War, innocent above
All raptures Elysium brings, we must
Bid our adieus from our affairous lust.
Our love's as the sun: warm in our tenders,
Fresh with fire, finding various figures
In thund'rous puffs that make our grounds wet;
But as the world's stage goes, the sun must set
From man's earthy scene to proceed another.
By Hymen, know you I've a lover
And I must stay true. Beg not my love
Or use soft breast or lips to make a move;
If you do, we'll have another day,
And by the mourning, I'll beg you to stay.

The Masquerader

I put on an image or blissy airs
To shield the bosom of mine discontent
From Life's depressing sword, as I would not
Further to be attacked by the wielder.
As Life lives on, I'm confused of his shapes,
His strengths; the nature he puts before me
Only comes pervert from its first Eden,
And whatever war I put on Life
To combat the tyranny of his stage,
I'm left pulped to pieces methinks I can
Grow formless willows from the sadden seeds.
I know not mine going, nor my true place,
So I act as another form of man
To keep on life without losing my stand.

A Man of Fortune

Once, my world was shareable to the clouds
With each of Heaven's wights gifting me reign
To mine own pleasure: I could meal apples
Without fearing for worms on the taste;
I could speak a lover's Latin to dames
And come off cupidly without much art
To take them out; I could arouse the earth
To a garden of Elysian delights
Without painting the stage. But now, my world
Is without those clouds, without those irrations
Of fear, as all my steps are with Nature
And decay each sweet nothing I've harbored,
And I know not who to cure this parley
If I carry to keep another day.

A Confession for a Millionairess

Verily, I'm a rat's ass of your mind,
Your income, or the dames you hire in kind
To believe your feeling; though you've achieved
All that a woman's supposed to conceive,
You're more as a shrewish Kate that deserves
A Petruchio's chastisement by your curves
Than one measure of poet's versèments.
You bark at opinions, take amusements
Away of all, & treat the working mass
With Holier-Thou soul in your class;
You confound at this reason, but I give ear
To your Damon and Pythias who fear
And think twice to relate your heart's meaning;
As if they do, they could risk you screaming.

Night & Day

No matter if the Sun chariots
The finest hour, or Dian's eye looks
On in darkness, my mind's eye fancies
Thy image of grace ere any spriteling
That presumes a fairy of our world's tale.
As the earth's pages turn, I'm with myself,
Without a true soul to flip the despair,
And it's but thy dream-like visage, the bliss
Thee inspires to love, & thy simple air
That but an art or the heavens can coin
To look on to keep me with the mettle
Of nature I'll be met with you once more,
As life keeps on its playing of woe
To separate keeps us for God's lonely show.

Ferrari Gran Turismo Omologato

Within mine full unartèd canon
Versed with measures without versing measures
And other contraries that dismiss its song,
Never have I ever hymned thee a praise
For thy full shape, thy fanciful color,
Or thy flamish speed that lust mine desire.
Thou art hast 'nough art to insight me
For thy cold creation; & as that
Statuer who had Love give life to his rock,
None shall prevail 'gainst us if you meet me
Halfway to permit my love on thy build.
O! may thy image live as Vinci's work!
As none compares to thee other than you
When thou art drives me as thou art drives true.

Garage 56 NASCAR: Chevrolet Camaro ZL1 – 24 Heures du Le Mans

Though mine verse is a twelve-month on the praise
And another French day race has made ways,
I still would to measure thee for thy make
And invention for drive, that, for God's sake,
None knew would out Le Mans the Le Mans
As king in thy class to all drifting pawns,
And end thy o'clock with most golden showers
Than the hypercars in their joven hours.
Pygmalions have given thee love
As they given thee life, & none above
Looked to fortune you out of thy presence;
For all unbirthèd eyers, I wish thee hence,
As thou art hast more art & drive for sport
And have bested the world's best racing court.

Alonzo the Brave to His Fair Imogine

As I horse on & be knight to our day
On propaganed lands that reason away
All grounds of mind for flesh & salary,
I would you special, my love, & merry
In mine come away, as well the return
With your image as green as the fern
Open to my back. You're but mine Love sent
I eyne to on this sphere of discontent,
Where paradise reads true & virtue stands
If the story's played. I would unpray mine hands
If you feel for a loose baron for lust
With mine away; so please, for 'Sake, be true
And forsake me not as fathering friends
As I war out for unlikely ends.

Loneliness Personified

I'm as that selling beetle, inconstant
With confused flesh, who tries to reap the buzz
Out of other latinated eyes,
But ends up inviting a scare to them
When mine presence is shown. Am I ugly?
Am I deformed? Am I gross? Do I creep?
Mine art's not to shoo off, but Adams
And Eves take me as if I'm no part of
Our God's offspring, & I know not the spec
That drosses them off like the black plague
In my fleaness. Wherefore the reason,
No ears have the buzz nor tongues have the race
Of my heart; for I'm merely a presence,
Desired to be dissolved with the past tense.

I, Tartuffe

I, Tartuffe, am a man of Narcissus,
And am no fool to our own precipice:
Steeped & balance of our own love for none
With all loves considered under the sun.
I tell my heart, yet my heart tells another,
Though mine heart doubts to question on a lover
Since the love may be other than mine own
That's well with love that grass & flowers hone;
I have nat'ral face & hold up a glass
To bring to health all that may drink alas;
I love, & toast by it to love no love
And allow what may that permits above;
I am Tartuffe, though I'm not what I am:
For I love the sheep to speak as a lamb.

Adonis' Note to His Venus

Thy hearts for me exceeds many with love
With it to only like heavens above,
But methinks thy nature is excessive
And takes love away than thou wills to give,
Cringing my bosom's weight of your too-much
In heaviness that begat from thy touch.
I wish to please, but it will seem a lie
When thou art expects Love's railroad ties
Off a loose train of me, while I'm unseasoned
To thy love that sees my blood untreasoned.
And our time with love has been a minute,
So let us come away of love's profit
We envision with rings, & sleep on us,
So our nothings can be sweet & not bust.

Sextus Tarquinius, First Perspective

If I go with this, I pawn mine honor
For a king, & trade the lode of reason
For musty dirt & vain rivers of lust,
Forsaking myself for myself's desire.
I'm with what's writ, but my naked armor
Shields not the bows of Love that quiver me
With attacks, & gives knocking at my ribs
That erupts a lewd lava to my heart
And flames mantle of my brittle conscious.
In that face I love, I saw a heaven,
With virtuous angels doving her cheeks;
I know not if I'll see this dream again,
And if I do, I'll have to patient my youth
For death, to see if spheres are worth our truth.

On the Zeus at Olympus

The world's wonder of Phidias hand,
Zeus, Olympus-bound, reigns as he sits
Mighty in figure, with man's manument,
With the staff of Victory in one arm
And Assurance eyne guiding man to truth.
Glorified is he as Attica's best
And Cronos conspired son, as he powers
The quakes of Tellus to shiver the earth,
Can make thunder from his own cloud & airs,
Dry up the grand earth-shaker from water,
And fate out other gods fates to his fortune;
And by this statue, Zeus is made for man
To give understandment of the heavens
In the grand nature & wonder of life.

On Pericles Funeral Oration

With thunder-verse in phrases lightning-like,
Pericles orated Lament himself
Upon a sorrowous public in war,
When Hope seemed abandoned as they entered
A Hell more fraught of Hades influence.
We've been met with other greatnesses with verbs
In similar times, as that of Gettysburg
With our states divided; but to give witness
On this speech through Thucydides prosings
In our age amazes me with freshness
The speech portrays, as if 'twere baked this week,
And the endurance it's given to statue;
And I hope through my small verse I praise it right
So others will distract darkness for light.

About Nothing

I'm nothing, & but image of the verse
I muse from that possessive cloud's curse,
That jails one to finish his product
When his art is painted, who keeps me rut
Of life: Saturn-like & begone with mirth.
But since you're human as you're of the earth,
I give you my soul on a plate to mark
And poke out argument of my true hark,
Hoping you'll see me as prose before verse,
As my translation is same, & a terse
To a few words for all understandment
When it seems my muses aren't human sent.
For this is me as I'm returned to dust
As all, with Time to decide my verse to bust.

The Great Fire of Rome

By Nero's fate or not, Vulcan's empire
Conquered & reigned 'gainst the powers of Rome
To remind the books of another Troy
In likes of an Alex, to revent ground
The Latins stood on for a gothic age.
The flames cared less of youth, lesser of sex,
Nor if salt of the earth fought with pepper;
For only Nature took its worst course
And studied human folly for ego
To deconstruct man's spirit by the rib,
Leaving most coughed up by the tongue of heat
And spat out like a mucus of sickness;
And it was nothing the Romans had seen
As eyes were then open to Heaven's mean.

Abraham, Sacrificing Isaac; First Perspective

For my Lord, I'll sacrifice mine best end
To obtain what He would of me to mend,
So His name shall glory around nations.
I'll do with love & lose my attractions;
But here, my challenge faced is beyond me
That looks closer as poison than God sees
In sacrificing my son for His truth.
The simple act is plain, as with virtue ruth,
But there's a struggle in my heart that doubts
Against this giving, as it seems more for clouts
Than for heaven. But something too whispers
At my soul to trust this evening's vesper,
And for my God, methinks this is Thy voice,
With faith & hope in Thee to love this choice.

Moses, First Perspective; A Study

Without word of mind, nor book at the heart,
God hast divined me with His manned wisdom
Near burning trees that sat with Mount Sinai,
Posting up the past & futures of earth
And its detriments, reigning down His law
To help the fate of man to his garden.
But in His thunder-depth voice that shook me
With clearness of truth, I know not translation
Of it to recent words for understandment;
For it's revealed to me, but I may struggle
In revealing to a hopeless public
The heavenal truth midst of suffering…
I ask my true brother not to doubt me,
But help in my tongue that overclouts me.

Julian the Apostate, First Perspective

I'm not the ass disguising as lion,
But lion as an ass for sakes of this herd
I've been born to: obeying Prudence law
By the necessity of life to live,
But embracing reason's trite to have truth
When this herd becomes the ass of itself.
For the lion strikes not at every ass
Of ears, but waits his time to have his day;
And though knowing this world's loss of saneness,
I must have smarts on my attacks, unless
I wish a smart ass to make ass of me
When I'm ill-prepared for his foolish takes;
So allow me this disguise as an ass
So I'll know the fool better than the mass.

Julian the Emperor, at the Apollo of Daphne; First Perspective

As a youth, & at the crown of my reign,
This land of a paradisal vain
Excites me for red color in the face;
But, as king, I must preserve manly chaste
To permit not my heart before reason
In chasing spells, as did Jupiter's son
When blinded for Daphne. But indulging
This land of perfumes would halt my heart's pulsing,
Trammeled by the art of war's oppression,
To relief me to my imagination,
Having all desires. I'm with all successes
A king could have! but again, the acts please
No Plato, nor Cicero, who I rank,
And wish imitate on my virtue's tank.

The Hippodrome of Constantinople

The chariots race between blue & greens
As if the horses were taking sons
Away from the earth to revive them again;
Thus was the scene of this Roman circus.
But this seat of the republic, though fun,
Realized the corruption of decayed Rome
By this Anastasius reign. We witness
Law silent under the cloth of circus
With Avarice at his best to poison:
Reason's mar wished to sword the innocent,
Wives were made unwively by a brother,
Boys were kidnapped, and daughters preyed upon,
With men without will to make will of their lust.
The circuses were nice, but portrait to Rome,
And added to weak bread that was given
To sloth the people from their virtuous kin.

The Enchantment of Actaeon, Ere His Metamorphosis; First Perspective

As the moon escapes Zeus' puffed-up empire
To eye Nature's children strait in the dire,
My sights worship this huntress of beauty
To its tender form, along this white tree,
As she bathes in ponds worthy of Neptune
That clears freshness ere the summers of June.
My innocence of youth may scare her sights
As I like a lion before his fights
Into his prey; but my purpose is new
And clear from intent, as I'm quivered, true
From love, but to discover her mystery
If she would arrow back her love to me
And know I'm filled with it to her pureness,
As no other is founded with her bliss.

The Enchanted Hubris of Icarus; First Perspective

I fly, upon soaring skies & wonder,
Where destiny has no destination
Save ventures in her plans, Mount Parnassus
The only verse to mine enchantment,
And my father's vision limits my dream
To see the conquership of Zeus' empire.
I forget his tales of old for my youth's age,
The only heart of me that whispers compass,
For direction I should take- And it speaks
Me to further the sun, Apollo's reign,
So I may reach flight of muse never seen!
My eyes imitate the gloss of the sun,
And I'm full innocence to what I am-
Watch me now grace the sun as a- dove!

Cid Hamet Benengeli,
The Mahometan Philosopher
(A Study on the Humors)

The child-fancy that the luck of the earth
Will fate out its condition as it's worth
Is at the hat of delusion for caps;
For all seems as a circle, taking laps
On Fortune's wheel, without hope of renewal,
Save upon that life that's with endless rule
In God's kingdom, & likens to seasons
That change beyond that of Nature's reasons,
With all states of the world soon to vanish
As the fed will die with the hungered famish.
We must attach to nothing, even nothing
Itself, so we may hear heaven's music ring
When we're away of the earth's bread & wine,
Filled with nothing to please our cup's grapevine.

Thomas

With all my works, with all my seasons passed
To sacrifice, with all the mass I've massed
For a wafer, there's always a doubt in me
My life will never eye beyond this tree
That's my life: so rigid in form for growth
Though to young of birth for an apple's youth.
Wherefore comes these whispers as the serpent,
That leads of no good but for evil's lent?
Do I sacrifice too much of mine life
Where I have no enjoy beneath the strife?
My doubting doubts futile on these questions,
But still reign me as loving affections,
As I know not if I'll be met good
By them, or if I'm trailing in a hood.

An Affair to Remember

Our affair was one for the books in love,
How our verses tied like hands to the dove
Of spirits, though our acts quivered with hooves
That were too cloven & french to fill louvres,
And how our passions had better marriage
Than most settled with the baby carriage.
For this affair was rebel on love's law,
Though Cupid's mother & he made our flaw
To excite much of our lover's passion
When our star-crossed ways met to our fashion.
Though we must part for our better conscious
To not let our affair make us cautious,
This love will always remember me
As love's clouds were nice to tender me.

For Dulcinea Del Toboso, From the Perspective of Don Quixote

'Gainst better judgment that helps our last days
And that heaven's rule that keeps us with God's ways,
I persist mine love to find that Elysian face,
That no heaven nor hand hast made more chaste,
Through furious ventures in Orlando's trade
Who was knighted in love to any raid,
And tough out any hurt beyond human
That minds deadly & other slothy sin.
I know not this love, but love's mystery
Guides me as Hercules through misery
To find out if my mind's eye true to see
Her beauty's bosom, clear & blemish free,
Or if I'm taken fancy by no muse
To see true matters take mine love to use.

Mount Parnassus, A Study

Upon Parnassus, great muses reign light
With generation & verses to sight,
To inspire all to greatness with heaven
From man's condition in days of seven:
Apollo lyres next to Clio for song,
Euterpé graces take the lyrics along;
Our Thalia makes us laugh with the verse,
While Melpomene sads us with its curse;
Terpsichore indulge us dance with our hearts,
Erato muses will to praise our parts;
Sacred Polymnia verses well
With Urania of the stars to tell,
As Calliope gives reign on all epics
And husbands the ones best with iambics.

The Last Supper, A Study

For as these days conceit themselves to last,
I'll be cruxed to a cross, as good men fast,
Upon grounds of bad truth and burning
Confounded by Satan's pleasure to sing.
But worse, a devil will betray me
Who's one of mine; and the worser I see,
My Peter, will thrice reject me and doubt
As the rooster crows and takes his flight about.
But, upon this last supper, I break bread
That thou shalt eat: for this is my flesh,
And of this wine, my blood, thou shalt have drink;
And thee will keep this of mine remembrance,
Until the earth is brought to mine essence
With our Kingdom to come in transcendence.

Roxana Venus; First Perspective

Cupid, hold thee this mirror to my love
So I can pleasure to please all natures-
Is mine bosom fair, mine teeth as ored pearls,
Mine skin as silk for heavens to beam me?
What of mine eyne? See them as the nearest sea?
Or the mouth? As ripe as forgotten fruits?
Oh! The trouble we women fight over
In looks, so our marred lover may be pleased!
But, Cupid, this is our nature's debt
To please the man, as men go out for wars
To protect us women from hot Trojans.
But, I hope my lover of war will please me,
As this mirror from my face test my soul
To desire, for a love to fill my hole.

Saint John the Baptist; First Perspective

Father, I've submitted to Thy Spirit
And have shepherd to sheep along pastures;
Thou hast purposed me within Thou greatness
But methinks the Messiah is to come
Greater than me. I see him without sight,
And behold him, though he's without our touch:
For he's to restore things as the garden
That gave happy to our first parents,
Ere the serpent seduced them to wrong fruit.
For I'm not he, nor am I Elijah;
But if it be in Thou Spirit for me
To lead this Messiah as the chosen one,
I submit as the shepherd to this lamb
To resolve the world from that wrathful ram.

Salvator Mundi, First Perspective; A Study

Father, Father; why hast thou forsaken me?
These contrary Romans who've taken me
Cross me, & hold me to crucifixion
From offense I've caused them, without fiction,
In the calling you've purposed me on earth
To wont all to Thy Kingdom for their mirth.
In this Pilate age with Tiberius times
All are confused of justice with their crimes,
And for this, I believe it's the devil
Who warps man to think to kill is civil.
But, why must I go as this? My Father,
Maybe you wish me for something greater;
And for this, I'm open arms to thy trust
As these flames are no match to the earth's rust.

The Ganymede

A blessed hero & Heaven's wine-bearer,
The soul of youth object to affection,
Thou graces me with love in thy bigness
Those three beauties hold no space to make,
And send me muse when my sword is poor
From natures that abuse me of lyring.
By the planet of all planets, thy space
Is few; but through me, there's an exception,
As with you, I'm with higher forms of love,
And eye thee for thyself in thy command
Of not being small nor taking light tenders
As a woman to trick them for honors;
And of this, I permit thee with this praise,
As most muse not my end in these last days.

The Suppliant; First Perspective

I gave mine all, yet I'm but nothing;
I've played all tricks of my trade for something:
Approached verbs of applied wisdom as wise,
Handed vice for virtue in Nature's lies,
Taken all sin as sloth, & doubted acts
That were wanton for fame, & thought facts,
But each number that I've list to add me
Has done none but confuse & subtract me
From true soul, & the path of mirthy gifts,
In where it's to be found, on earth's drifts,
Manna, in these reigning hungers of life.
I plead Fortune to forgive me in this strife,
As she tells us not our mystery through fate
Nor if suffering will soon lack its hate.

The Golden Ass

As my sonnets' verse, lies there a golden ass,
That takes mouth to lick up the flow'rs & grass
From all anointment from dust & earth,
Without a world's care for humanal mirth.
Though this ass is mere show as the rest,
Men lust for this ass for their interest best
In hopes they'll reach the top of Fortune's wheel
And come away with O's they'll never feel.
But, as of late, this lust has become more,
As in these times, men will do all for
A golden ass: even gouge their mother's wombs
To see their origins for the ass's fumes,
Even though the golden ass is mere ass
As our other lust that gift us with alas.

The Reflections of Tiberius Caesar, First Perspective

If I knew my writes, or the how of it,
And what to leave unwritten at present,
May all forces that conceit the heavens
Visit me more fire on my wretched sins
Than what these sevens bring on suffering.
My character is ill, & ails from changing,
As I'm jailed to my tyrannous senses
That fault & doubt me from Fortune's chances,
And I've no fate but that in fate itself
That I've grounded in disgust of myself.
Any movement, or any finger lacked
Of my knows, is bound to be found & hacked,
And disgraced me by what's set of my soul
I habited in youth to a useless toll.

The Doubt of the Artist, or
The Renaissance Man; First Perspective

With these world's pangs that fight against my will
To bring life to a seed to test the times,
With water & nurture as the first tree,
To despite good & evil unto thought
And let peace be beckoned to innocence,
I know nothing, & seem far of myself
To a deluded curse brought of some god
I went to when my eyes were of the clouds.
Every conviction, each clause & maxim
I take line to antiquity's finest page,
But mine art is challenged for doubt by nature,
Leaving me to shadows for truth in this life
And in wonderance if I'm mad for genius
In these clouds suffered by a - pajock.

The Bald Adulterer, First Perspective

Ye men of states & all heavened empires,
Keep thy consorts safe, but thy wits with eyes,
As their come lies a bald adulterer
That runs & vices the streets for his best end,
With sweet nothings on his tongue for ears
To seduce & lie thy mate for what he wants.
You may laugh him out buildings for his look,
But women, for men, careless of his face
And more for his pow'r, & Hercules vain
He purports with courage by his tongue's game.
He also can take men, if that be his thing,
And leave the fight for the couple after him;
And I want this to all ere he takes to thee
As his baldness was in surprise to me.

David, Before Goliath; First Perspective

The Lord hast inspired arks to take on rains,
Enrapt towers to confuse them of names,
Hast given heart of those in lonely blood
And below dust when earth molds them to mud,
But 'gainst this prouder giant, with words
That reign more than his acts to boast herds,
Will God help me feat of him in this fight
That none have fought in feet to glore His light
To halt this baalic soul of his conceit?
I've but stone & sling to my bone's meat
To have this champ, with mine head to the skies.
I know not of my lay, if I'm in lies,
But from the Lord's pow'r, I'm for the future
As God helps those of a faithful nature.

The Imaginary Invalid, First Perspective; A Study (A Study on the Humors)

I'm sick, & think myself to a disease;
By stitous truths, I've been lack without ease,
And me fears my soul's itch may lead a scratch
Greater than mine own disposition, which
Would give the gods the control of me,
Without mine own hand of man's herb to see
Me well, fating a hades to my heart
With other hells I've no fire to set apart.
Others claim me out my head, but they
Have no eye to my inner wars that may
And keep me of life to the trust of folk,
Who claim themselves learned as their eyes are woke,
As I feel that aging death upon me
Without a skin's wrinkle to claim life's fee.

Phaedra Atychos, First Perspective; A Study

For love of this reigning sun, I'm the sea
With arky salts that drift & disturb me,
Rivering a dark & wailed lake of tears
For divineness his light shows to my fears.
For he resembles manly soul of olds
With youthy lust Fortune favors in bolds;
I want this, but know my lack shouldn't love,
As it can present ill-fate from above
From overwanting, thus pushing it away.
But my heart evapes from this burning May,
Wishing my will of waves to take over
And possess this son by any power.
I fear me, as I'm apart of nature,
And may follow love, not my mind's mature.

Samson Agonistes, First Perspective

Alas! Whose agrievement ever been mine?
My troubulous heart's without word to line
The fate I've been strung too by sick Fortune,
Who's without eye for men, except her son.
I was lauded Nemean-nerved for strength
To take any guys for the midst of length,
But, for purpose my devil's will hast known,
I was taken by a harlot's vamped moan
And left to her will, by visions of me
Taken to peace & ease she could make be.
But with seduce, she cut mine seven hairs
That were the all of mine strength in affairs,
And left me nothing than with stones above
I'll topple me with, as I've fooled with love.

Polinka Saks, First Perspective

I opened my wife to arts beyond art
And other gift of scripture that have heart,
But by my niceties, I was lied to
As she lied with a lie to abide to
Another with love & without constraints,
That gave her arrows away of her pants.
But once her lie got the best of her,
She thought twice, & regretted her lie's purr,
And was cat to me & was a kitten
For milk, wishing forgiveness from her smitten.
She confessed her lie & remembers her age
And reminds me the sweet truth I did sage,
But I know not if she's still true in this lie
As she may be still lying & still cry.

Vincent Van Gogh: A Lust For Life; First Perspective

Rejected by peers, rejected by arts;
I'm reject if rejection had a name!
As this confractured earth rounds without me,
I find me at a lust of life's tenders.
But in this, I'm alone for its beauty,
And fear my canvas will wont to retrace
The wherefores of my mind's eye as nothing,
And have not my enspirited image,
As the vulgar mock my impressions
And lower them to no understandment,
And laugh as they know not of a sun's trace.
I'm not an Aeneas who can first Rome,
But hope by graces beauty will find art,
As I'm ready of mine own soul to part.

Titus Latinius, First Perspective

A nourished dream was angeled unto me
Under direction, as the future sees,
For me to speak truth against nature's crimes
And get games going that please gods of rhymes;
But I've avoided tales for suspicion
As I doubt this importance to fiction.
But since I've had the dream, I spoke no truth,
And feel, to my worst content, ill & at ruth
To a muridious & slothful will
That has an ail to progress me & kill.
Maybe the dream's right, & not special,
Telling me what's man if he has the mettle,
As I avoid my luck to a better gift
By forsaking truth for a tiny spiff.

The Death of Lucretia; First Perspective

I clutch to this sword for my salvation
For shame of mine heart, now raped & defiled,
And wish to be maid with my sins & end them
To venture for better life without this
Mortal failure. I'm done with doubt to fates
As the heavens are more apt to this space,
And finished with all the victim of me
For other bodies to advantage me
Without consent; & as planets move me,
I'm consented to make life out of life
And play roles of my own choosing with strife.
A Roman's death for a man is woman,
So allow me to permit this nature
And thus commit my death for this picture.

The Nigerian Prince, First Perspective (A Study on the Humors)

I'd depreciate it, from the top of my heart
You'd send me checks, off the level, to start
My campaign against the world, from Thebes
To the flights of Memphis, giving my leaves
On the ones who reperialized to dust
My people, and imbirthing a new trust
Of land, so we may enjoice a new world
That's with the old lease of life, and make
The world one pole apart from the earth's shake.
Alas, take it out for my wife, whose
Rabbit cried, so we may cash it in twos,
And be on our merry day in this earth
And on our way to conquering our mirth;
And in your help, with the money you send
We'll fall on the phone as you make your amend.

The Englishman in Moscow

They're many masters yet few margaritas
To share & to be sold, but by Gargantua's
Tongue I've seen it all: a cold world for warmth
As men rejoice in faces of no mirth,
Marching forth like dust poured off lifeless clays
Without spirits to compare out the days.
But by Jove, good heavens! There's the train ride!
And another, keeping the civil's pride-
The flags, banners, colors & rests above
Are willed to live as life ceases to love;
And there's the devil, that cat pistoled up,
And the temperance of birds all whistled up;
I hope I'm enjoyed of my trip later
As I quiver all touch by this paper.

The Portrait of Captain Ahab, First Perspective

From the leg to the top of mine person
I'm oppressed, & see without vision
The seas of me I command like Jonah,
To no end out on this gourdic coma;
For it insanes me to blood revenge
On this whale, as it did me in no linge
That reasons itself justice on my life
To find any cause to against me in strife;
But it seems the more I lose heart with Mars,
I'm made to darkness by the brightest stars,
That consult me to reason out matters
When my passions leave as its own masters;
But they've left twice, as I'm now made sick
To this only chant: Death to Moby Dick!

Timon of Athens: the Misanthrope; First Perspective

How shall I verse? Simple, all that man sings
In hate, with the whole nine to nature things:
Men that merry themselves in no merry
But put themselves out to chase Love's fairy,
Women that lie their face to every lie
And save to all heart, as the good pass bye;
Men who profit & profess civil change
Yet civil to no greed as powers range,
Women who play innocent for a face
To have Love see blind to her bows as chaste;
Men who fall in a fountain of themselves,
Women who have whorship of their own veils.
This is of my hate; but though I'm no stand
To humans, I'm still sawn to states of man.

Behemoth the Cat; First Perspective

Mistake me not for something pretty:
For I'm ugly as they come; note my profile:
I'm a silent trance that hinds on two legs
And imitate poor beggars in his begs,
My fur is shoddy for any magic
To stop my tongue's habit to bathe & lick,
My eyes are shot but lack the blood of them
As I make ready next victims to limb,
And the moon's grace for background is facade
To my soul, as virgins hunt on their hide.
But, with my looks, people play the fool
And love deceivement by my picture's tool,
And give me my wants within their lacking
As I play innocent to this play's macking.

The Discreet Charm of a Bourgeoise, From His Perspective

My desires are my will; and if mine wills wrong,
I'm without rights to them! I spend whatever
And follow Theleme's code of what I will,
Whether it be in designer or trends,
To please the soul of me without a soul
And love myself as no one's business.
Offend me not: I'm as a poet and
Sensitive to all of Nature's touches;
And leave critiques for the lesser than broke
As they need the love to have a nice flex.
But alas, why must life be so cruel? I'm proud
And deadly to sin as this world's victim,
But I hope as Epicurus servant
I'm able pay merry for this world.

The Portrait of Mildred Pierce, First Perspective

I've given myself up for my business
And have added sweat & tears for a bliss;
But though I'm woman to a woman's age,
I'm trammeled alone to this manly cage
I've honed myself in imitating men,
Without a mirth in the world to this sin.
For I'm without a mother's son to part
Us by death, with my thicker blood of heart
To cringe at the calling of me & I,
As I've made too-much team of my own tie.
Success is sweet, but what's it without love?
I gave no time to those cupids above;
And now that I'm made for the fleeting dust,
Heavens save me not from my earthly lust.

The Portrait of Thomas Gradgrind; First Perspective

I'm a man of Realities & Facts
And known to Statistic in his own acts,
And without any sense for our spheres,
As they're made to without sense by my peers
And without article to proceed them fact
That the convince of them is not an act.
I take no art, nor the creative people,
As man's imagination was built evil
And cannot sense out the more that's on earth
Than what's dreamed of in their forsaken mirth,
But take the man of coldness to the fact
As he's able to see before his act,
To keep the condition of life human
Without a force to opposite my kin.

Angel Eyes

Excuse me while I disappear to drink
And confound my thought to what I may think:
Life has begotten me of angels,
But spits me to roaring lions & angles
That tempt me sober from its vigilance
And all spirits that help for merriments.
The poor aren't with me: I'm poorer than they,
With each to his own sadness & his say;
And a friend is without me with these times
To prove loyal, when friends are hard to find.
I've lost mine angels eyes to pointlessness
To eye every corner a death to bliss,
And I know not where these spirits will sink,
But excuse me while I, disappear…

Self Portrait, with a Friend

We are two. Another fool, makes we three…
But unaside the jokes, my friend's of me
As Pythias was to Damon in Greek,
With a trust that's within each other's meek.
But, at times, methinks I'm the lesser friend
And feel I'm not at mine to please his end,
As he's always there when our earth's around,
And will give me life if furries surround.
So I try best to satisfy his need
When Hell's high waters come from Neptune's lead;
But he says I've done enough on his end
That's worthwhile on our friendship's amend;
But I hope his tongue matches his language
As he's the best friend I praise in passage.

A Habit With Me

Every lover's kiss, every Cupid's bow,
Every echo of narcissus below
Seem to be Love opposite of our age
And weird lyrics for a popular page:
For you enter me different soul for heart
And pray our love are never poles apart.
And I've doubt the many thought of leaving
As many love made me fear its keeping;
But of this earth in its independence,
Love is needed more on its dependence,
And with your love's offer, I'm made to love
That'll never leave me for the other dove.
Your clutches are tender, founded to warm,
And habits me to stay from this world's storm.

The Letters

LETTER V

Dear Susie,

I received your message of recent and will decide myself to respond through Word form. You ask me if I could introduce you to my pop star friend Tito, but because of your beggarment and desperatisms, I will decline your request. However I can report you some insides about this honeybunch you look up to so you can discuss it with a hardcore Tito fanclub or share it with your friends so you can make it up to them you've been in Tito's company:

First off and most importantly, I've seen Tito in the shower and I must say that the left side of his body is shattered. His leg gives way and his skin is wrinkled prematurely from all the fumes he makes with himself. His head can at times turn all the way around, as if he were an all-seeing Janus or Brahma, and he can poke out his eyes as if he were an owl for his prey, and sometimes he combines this as if he were in some modern warfare of the night in trying to find the killer to make a 360 noscope on him. And if you notice his hands, the thumbs turn out and his index fingers are zig-zagged. You relate your affections in saying he's the most gracious man you've ever seen, but if you look at him close he's a bad looking man.

I'm pretty sure you're aware of his drinking, and I'll let you know he has been known to go to sleep and wake up the following year. So if you ever catch him in his merriments with drink, you do risk of him not speaking to you for a long time. And never ask to drink his drink: if you do you risk blowing up and being shot to the moon and being one with Selene. He does smoke a lot, and doesn't plan to give it up: he likes to drop the ashes on himself and pretend his underwear is on fire. You can try to 'save him' all you want, an expression woman of our day use when they see some blind goodness in a badboy they're attracted to, but he will not transform into this Clark Kent from the Superman you seem him as. He is his own man, and I know this because he tells me time and time again 'I'm my own man'.

You asked me if I thought he was talented, but I'll tell you the truth. Tito has a great gift: he has no voice or humor, but makes a great deal of money, which I think is a gift in itself. I like to call it Let's Confuse The Public as his talent. He has great strategy with all of his music, and has several connections with Influencers online. He works with all the biggies and knows Lil' Suck personally, and he pays several others to dance his song and to make it trend. Most of the time he strikes it big, and he makes the song get on the Top 20 on the Billboard. But this isn't enough in his eyes, so he pays more for positioning in the top 10 so he can have more time to be a Narcissus in the fountain and tell me how great and influential of an artist he is, with we to be punched with his music on the regular, not because people like it but because he has millions to keep it running on the radio. And since his sounds will make trends, influencers could care less to like the music: as long as it gets them pay from dancing to awful songs, then they're good, and as long as it gets other people views and attention, the song is fire in their ears.

And you ask if he is in the mood to marry. I'll tell you, from the amount of divorces he's been through and all the other female pop stars he's been with, I think you won't stand a chance by him since Tito has married thrice and has been with every woman possible of every figure and proportion and, in my opinion, will marry, if he decides to do so, some sort of an animal, nothing human, to put a smile on his face. At the very least it won't be anything human, maybe one of those robots made in Japan with exaggerated bosoms and enchanted souls to be under the direction and authority of everything the man commands it to, since Tito does have a problem with women being lazy in his house with no order and the independent types, yet still beg him for money and the finer things. He tells me all the time how psychotic women try to sleep with him only to be set for life and have him pay their bills of his riches, or how the same women only are around him just for Instagram or to get courtside seats at basketball games. I also expect him not to marry you because of the divorces that have ran him out of every cent and all of the expenses he pays for, and because you have no particular ability going for you other than your looks and your comedy that has made your dog bark a couple of times. At least his last wife was talented: she can put a cigarette in her navel and make it puff.

But with all of his riches and fame, he finds himself lonely and off, even though he has plenty of friends that he calls false because of his upbringing. For his last birthday he didn't invite anyone from the notion that everyone is fake, and sat in his living room listening to Ravi Shankar while singing happy birthday to himself. I remember one night I invited him to a UFC match, but he texted me how he couldn't make it because he got under the weather; but the next day when I related to him the Anderson Silva match, he told me the real reasons for his tardiness was because his hair didn't lay right, and his personal rule with himself is that if his hair doesn't lay right he won't go out. I wanted to do something special for him once upon a time and one evening I went to his house and I gave him a doll to give to one of his daughters, but he told me that he never gave it to her and stayed in his room and tickled it. I didn't know why he would rather tickle a doll meant for daughters when he has a spectrum of women waiting to hear back from him on Instagram and on iMessage, but I gave him a pass since he's a popular star and is excused for his eccentricities. I just hope it doesn't evolve him into thinking he's a Peter Pan and he starts inviting kids to his Neverland.

And don't fear the account I give you: every opinion I have related has been shared to his ear, which is a reason why he doesn't talk to me like he used to and I probably have no good chance of introducing you to him. And if you still fear these comments not private, a few weeks ago he put the cell phone conversation we had either on Instagram or Twitter where I gave him my heart and I had a gang of his hardcore fans hit me up and debate me about his greatness as a pop star. I didn't respond to any of them, but you can see how this idol worship is very prominent in our age as little teenagers and teenagettes get offended over a bit of reality I tell their favorite pop star. And fear not if these comments come off as vicious: I know he thought once I was the most warmest man he's been around and that's the reason why I'm in his most trusted company, but understand he says this because he doesn't see me as a threat and I'm not as popular as he. He knows I drop releases of my own, and knows they aren't doing so well, and I believe he just needs someone to be around so he can feel superior to calm himself of his nerves about his future. But when I do pass him in popularity and wealth and fame, which I will, I will definitely be hiring him to do the laundry, be my driver, and speak fluent Japanese just in case a samurai cop is on my tail from all the sizzurp I drink when I acquaintance myself with other artist.

So in closing, don't ask me to introduce you to him. You only contact me once out of the year and I won't follow up with your request. You also are annoying and distract me from making my own music. How about considering changing your name to Karen instead of Susie. You act like one, and highly doubt a flea would want to introduce themselves to you from your ridiculous directions. Figure out your life, and I hope this reaches your hands and eyes sooner than later.

Your friend,
Jeremitrius DeAngelo Cunnins

LETTER VII

Dear Sonya,

I come in peace, and I approach you without a malice vein in my bone. I understand you're mind is up and at em in all the conceited images you portray to your mind's eye of your husband being with other women, but I can assure you that during our trip to Yugoslavia your husband was a pure Ulyssess on his trip: fighting in our Trojan War helping us film content for our TikTok, while also destroying temptation along the way by rejecting many a Circe and Calypso while we went out to differing bars and clubs, so he may return to you, a virtuous Penelope, as a good man. We discussed business, and that's that. Sure, he praises the attitudes of European women when he's at the house, preferring the gentle sweethearts of Europe compared to a contentious hellcats that America produces, but he is only saying this because he, like a poet, compares you to this European summer's day and sees their virtue in your heart's content. Plus, he thought of you constantly, as he kept telling me that while we were out. I thought of my wife too. All of the guys on the trip thought of their wives, constantly. We all thought of our wives constantly and never even thought about the act of cheating or did such of the like. May I be paralyzed now, God forbid, if I lie.

LETTER VIII

Dear Darius,

I got your mixtape yesterday, and I listened to it earlier today. You wanted me to give you feedback because of my conversance in our pop music from the 20th century all the way till now. If you want the truth, I'll tell you: I love everything about it. It sounds great, looks great, feels great, tastes great, and just all in all great; but you do have one problem: you sang your lyrics in English. I think maybe if you would have sung your lyrics in French or Korean, then your music would sound a lot better; but since it's set in English, not only do I have to listen to your profanities in the measures, but I also have to hear the vulgarity of your voice. If your music was played for a man robbing a woman, I can guarantee the song would make them both look up. You have a voice that's not trained, without lesson, and it shows so much while you sing. I've no more criticism, but consider me.

Your honest friend,
Marion

LETTER IX

Dear Hastings,

I thank you for the consideration of allowing me to be a part of your business team, but quite frankly I could care less to make passive income. I understand I could retire early from accomplishing this feat, but why would I want to retire at 30? Unlike you, I actually like working at my job and need not be shamed by you or some other bloke that approaches me in a Barnes and Noble while I read my Marvel Comics into making extra. I mean, just the other day I was reading The Amazing Spider-Man with his adventures against that green Doctor Octopus when this half-mind from UTA cut me off from my strips and said Hey, have you ever thought about selling comics? No, I said. Well, he said, have you ever thought about selling anything in general? No, I said. And after rejecting his questions, this bloke proceeded on his secular testimony in how once he was a monkey for the streets sleeping with a least one different girl each day and reaching the success of sleeping with 50 women before he turned twenty, doing drugs like all his favorite rappers, picked it up a notch by sleeping with even more women when he made it to college, found himself a sinner and went to church one day and met a man by the name of Ace, aged 30, who approached him asking the same hyperbolic doubts he asked me and told him how he was retired. He asked him How did you get retired at 30? Ace chopped it up for about thirty minutes and they've been business partners ever since.

Abraham, which I believe was the dumbbell's name, which he didn't even tell me until he blew up my phone with text messages the next day about meeting him for coffee, continued on and said that after being with his mentor Ace for some time and meeting his other business associates, which all happened in the previous six months before I met him, he has become a changed man: he stopped seeing his main girl Ta'niffa and his side chick Becky and is now investing in himself, whatever that expression may mean to him, eats his breakfast at 3pm even though he wakes up 2 o'clock in the morning to get his day going, works out at 4 am instead of 6pm, goes to bed at 10 pm instead of 12, and not 7pm to get his full eight hours because he believes sleep is for the weak and he needs to give it up because he needs to prove himself he's really committed to the grind; he meditates for two hours daily, but told me how he wishes to pick it up because he wants to imitate and be the Dalai Lama as much as possible, listens to a new podcast each day, dips his body into a cold plunge, has a daily uncomfortable 'challenge' for himself which could either entail dedicating himself to acts such as screaming in the middle of a street in Dallas or running around Deep Ellum with his shirt off or making sure he has a conversation with at least fifteen new people each day to, as he told me, break away from the constraints of social anxiety; he also invests in crypto and the market, does dropshipping for three hours and calls his mentor Ace to talk to him for another three, takes long naps throughout the day that last from one to two hours, has become vegan after being shown a video of pigs killed from his partner Deb, watches no sports nor other entertainments, got rid of his TV, cut off five of his closest friends because he felt they weren't built for success like him and brought on negative energy, eats no breads, goes to no circuses, got rid of his Chevy for a Tesla to stop polluting the environment, got rid of all of his urban wear in exchange for business casual vetements, and now only uses subscription based services to get his toiletries as well as locking himself only to use but Postmates as well as UberEats to save time with his groceries and eating habits. He also tries to read a different book a day: not necessarily read a full book each day, but a page or two out of it; and with all of his extreme changes in his schedule, his main ambition is to retire by 23, and he's only 21.

With the amount of time he took out to explain me of his dreams, I had no doubt in my mind he would accomplish just that. He also told me how he was amazed and jealous how he met others making hundreds of thousands and they weren't even legal, and I believe this where I think he thought he had me, as he started asking me if my options were open. I didn't know what he meant if my options were open as I took it he was hitting on me after seeming to flaunt out his life's progress to then asking for my number. I reluctantly agreed to exchange contact to get him to go away. And two days after he followed up and asked if I wanted to meet up at Otto's Coffee to discuss business. I took it to be suspect so I just left him on read. And after a few days of this avoidance, he still texts me and calls me. As a matter of fact my phone is ringing now, but I'm not going to even look at the screen because it may lead him to wanting me to receive his cake or have him stick something extra up my stink, and I have to get it through your head that I wish not to receive the same from you.

I don't take you as a scam, as you told many plenty you weren't a scam, but I get annoyed, quite frankly, of the deluxe package of salesmen and women alike trying to pelt me with opportunities in making money and the world possessed with possessions. Everywhere I walk, every scene I set, every lyric I take to my ear, someone is speaking of money or the acquisition of it, and its lechery seems to be making everyone as these robots whose minds are programmed for the thoughts and work of money. With these people, I seem to be talking to hungry ghosts: entities with stomachs wide but necks narrow and consume waste to have it not satisfy their bellies, but not humans who are capable of more divinities in the acquirement of reason upon literature, philosophy, or other physical sciences as well as using the muses to develop in other such as painting or sculpture and the discussion thereof. Of course, many businessmen and women have plain intentions: willing to make money for their family or loved ones to provide and secure them for a future and better health;

but don't you think your family and loved ones would rather have your intentions set and planned in loving them and spending time, compared to being out all day long grabbing a bag that won't be enough as your ambitions for more get worse? That doesn't take money, that takes reason to rout your time for love. And plus, as our world turns and money becomes man's god instead of God Almighty Himself, your ambitions will worsen for money, as some isn't enough as first usage will open your eye to its corruption for power. And don't expect your loved ones to be away from this darkness: they will be the first ones to moneygrab and complain to you how you don't take them to the Cowboys game while your wife complains about you copping out of the Beyonce concert because your granduncle passed on. Or if you have broke cousins or uncles, they'll try to ask you every month to borrow, when you've already given them some they never paid back, and if you don't they'll shame you until you give it to them. I would do the same to you, they will say, and give you all the money in the world if I had it. Some family members will even pray for your death so your full account can be in their hands; at least this is what I've read or heard in some stories about the rich and famous.

I understand your intentions may seem clear of deception, but every cat looks innocent until you see its claws. And I understand your purpose with money may be in this like for the betterment of others' wealth, but give me boundaries: for we need not to get into business so quickly without knowing each other just yet. For your medicine to make me rich may not be for my servings, as you may deal out what you think may be beneficial to my health when, naive to the dosage, you give me a pill that may contradict the benefits of my soul. Even the doctor makes mistakes, so allow me to know you as for you to know me, to see if I'm as trustworthy and loyal to your standard as you are to mine: virtue's more important than making any buck.

Sure, it would be lovely to be able to make money while I lock myself in the bathroom with the radio on loud, but living under this money hungry earth disgusts me from even laboring for a cent. I understand the world is moving fast, as you as well as other business men have told me in their same lectures on money and I need to be ready in making more money before my job lets me go, and I won't be able to live in America with my income, but aren't I writing this letter to you now? I know you speak plenty on generational wealth, but do you really think your kids' kids' kids' kids' kids will continue to prosper? By the words of a historian, a state is born stoic but dies epicurean, and as states are built with man, I believe the same will happen to your futuristic offspring you constantly talk about. This same effect also happened to the greatest of kings, from the discussions of Polybius on the rise of the Roman Empire, and in the movement of their states: Rome was once held as a Republic, but then gave way to a senate and democracy, but fell to a dictatorship and continued to fall ever since. Regardless of the wisdom of our great ancestors, people will people, without anyone to have control over one man's decision other than himself for better or worse, and this is no exception to your family line. Do you believe the richest man in Babylon has his great grandson walking around a millionaire? One of those babes in the mix got too cocky and spent all the inheritance once he got it.

Forgive me if my thoughts proceed into frustration. I've carried these thoughts in my soul for some time, and you have triggered the full of them from your persistence in trying to get me to follow up with you. I do believe having an income is important, because I wouldn't be able to function in this life without it, but do I seriously have to invest every inch of my mind to the art of money? There's so much more richness to life than settling for riches. It's merely paper, and shouldn't be taken beyond that of a tool for fair exchange, and if you can't help me manage my finances then we aren't a good fit for each other. Life is suffering, regardless of the time period and how many times you tell me how much the world is changing and I need to make more money now, with the goals of it to trust in God and good wisdom, follow virtue, avoid vice, and add health, honor, and wealth only to make ease of life's troubles for a good life. You ask me Why not make millions? but I ask you Why? Why must I make millions if I don't have a good life? Why must I waste away for a buck if I don't have my health? Why would I waste away for green and blue signs if I don't have friends or a lady to enjoy it with? I send you this out of mere perspective, not something you should completely agree with, to understand me in where I come from and to halt your expeditious calls and texts that blow up my phone.

Your humble person,
Beastly

LETTER X

Dear Scorpion,

During our last sparring at Goro's Lair, you questioned me if I thought much of dying. Thou may make a mockery of me in mine sayings of this, but I was well in the thought of dying during our fights since you are well trained in thou art and have powers beyond what our masters above endow us with. But in this thought, there's no need to indulge in a womanish fear of it. I believe in following The Way we are well set for the afterlife, with our souls to be prepared for any battle that comes when our eyes meet their final close. But when I go, I don't want to be met with a malicious fatality: I would rather much be hit with an illness that gives me time to contemplate before I imitate sleep. People say they don't wish to suffer before they die; but thou art knows I'm not human, as I wish to know my dying hour, prologue it, and have my mind's book balanced before I give my final check out. Methinks mine soul will peace knowing I conquered myself before nature conquers me. I also don't want you, or any of our mortal kombat, to stand around me while I fall to the grave: I don't want Sonya to search me on the casket for money, I don't want Raiden to come away of my misfortunes, I don't want Johnny, even if a funeral is held, to dress up in the bath robes he wears as if it were nothing; I don't want Shang Tsung, our most valiant master, to try to transport my body out of the gravial system for his own operation to try to steal my soul, I don't want that son of Antartica Sub-Zero, whatever his real name is, imitate the same behavior and take my specimen to a freezing camp. I just wish to reflect in peace, have the doctor who feeds me take me off the oxygen pump if needed, and allow my soulless flesh be bred for the mixture of the dust while I'm transported to another dimension.

But in death, in following the way, methinks we can make humor in death; for example, if you died it would strike me as funny, because who needs you? Constantly flicking thy tongue with flames at everyone, and always having thy face under a mask but when released to eye on thy flesh man is horrified by the sight. I think if you died, it would save the world from ugliness, and we could be one more less of a cave in grotesquations.

This is my heart, and all the blood I put down for words. If I continue me, I'll twist my tongue for confusions. My actions will speak louder when we are close to death on our battlefield in fighting, but ye can be assured thou art will beckon the grave before I. I will see you on doomsday.

Your close friend but closer enemy,
Liu Kang

LETTER XIII

Dear Andy,

Stop complaining to me of your troubles with these 'modern' women. I'm tired of these spectrum-like letters of you constantly repeating yourself. Are you a case? If so, take a valium. You need to chill because with all of your contingency I bet it's not that deep. A woman is a woman, so I don't know why you're surprised of all the trouble they cause you. I understand you may be under a bad sign with trying to pick up the Venus of your fancy, but as you well know Fortune favors the bold, and methinks it's quite unmanly of your person not to devise between all of the options presented to you at our present utopia. For you must continue the fight in finding the one you love despite the confusion they may breed you in, as did Pantagruel when he was tired of his whorish ways with women, and be content with some of the chaos, because one good woman is enough to cure the ailments of ten dishonest dames.

To get this out the way, why are you even using all this money on women? After spending a thousand for a dating coach that treats you as one of his hoes, and after spending another grand on parlors and that woman called Happyness, I would think you would have enough sense to wise up from all this mess. The thousands you spent on these modern women could've been spent on investments or a business or your own intelligence, which you seem to need to cure from retardation, and by the next ten years, by finance and some luck of the imagination, you'll probably have all of those hoes you spent thousands on sleep with after you show them a thousand without spending it. Money is a funny item, and people seem to be seduced to the gravitational pull of it even though they may protest it as evil. Women speak of wanting a man out of the modern romance novel, who is sweet, generous, and is built for love, until they meet a man of some status and power and are automatically, in spite of themselves, submitted to his will because she feels protected under his empire. This should be of your understanding, and it's the money itself that gains the attraction, but the influence you have on other people with that liquid that keeps her along, and this stems from your quotient of knowing to the authority of your workplace position. You may be able to spend her with dolls, teddies, and other jewelry, but until you actually have her as your handmaid, then she will constantly abuse your person, remind you how insignificant you are, beat you because you make less money than her, and make you contemplate life in your unmanliness. I've seen many a man be sucked dry of every cent because he didn't understand part of this concept, as a rich man can be just as vulnerable as the poor with gold-diggerish women if he is not protected with his manliness. But what's the use in telling you this? You'll probably use this as another argument to incite your incelious attitude. And even with this, I wouldn't suggest you rigidly focus on making money, as you may turn into a corrupt asshead and start acting like these men we have to deal with on social media who are just as annoying as the women who bark about their problems. But because the man has money, people listen; as with the woman: because she is beautiful, people listen and praise every prose on her tongue as verse. It doesn't matter how much you know, people only listen to those who attract them. But this is neither here nor there.

You ever considered going for the operation? At least after the result would you conceit the privilege of a man by his arms, but also contain the privilege of a woman having men confused for your affections before you make love to them, as well have woman who may be a descendant from Sappho of Lesbos and cure your ever-aching desire. You could go to the nearest hospital, but they may check your mental state before giving you any blockers or following up with the surgery; so I recommend you go to Home Depot, go to the 'Hand Tools' section, and purchase the emergency sex change kit. I first heard about this unique device on the *Johnny Carson Show,* even though some foolishly use it to knock nails into wood. By abiding by this kit, not only would you be saving a fortune, but you'll also be saving time to help you knock on your own wood and be sexless in no time when you use it. And be sure to do this process in a restroom where no one is of your witness. This process will hurt, but the negatives out way the positives and you will be deconstructing all of these perceptions our society is so keen on doing, and all you would have to do to top off your newfound you is by going to the nearest Dollar Tree, but a Barbie dress and a wig, and wait out Downtown Deep Ellum to curb your enthusiasm. You would think there are laws against all of what you're doing, but our world stage is so confused and without the heavens above them that every scene and entrance is permitted, especially if you have someone recording your every step and a loud voice so you can be the next face of WorldStar.

Have you at least thought of exchanging your affections for a boy? When having one, you don't have to deal with quarrel all night, or have one nag on you for golden fleece, or complain to you how the Jason next door is the better argonaut than you, or demand you to engage the gasping chaos they hold their womanly feet on. With a lover boy, you'll be with one who has the same fleshly exigencies as you, and submissively follow your order because he knows that respect is very valuable to a man or power. And best of all you don't have to worry about being beaten, cucked, or robbed for all your pay even if he is under your wing, since may seem paranoid of that option I gave you of making the woman your woman.

Have you ever thought about getting a bath? It's another wonderful invention descended from our ancestors, and there's something out there called soap that you can use to, get this, clean yourself with. Have you ever taken a good whiff of your insides? When we last hung out at the Wonder Bar, you smelled like a walrus who swam in mud and slithered through a fan expo to hug all the nerds that were there. You are beyond musky, and one thing that women dig is a man's smell, and if you don't smell good, forget it. Or have you at least considered a good job? I understand you may disagree with the workplace politics, but if you are that desperate for love, you could abandon your future for a dizzy modern dame who has her own career; but, as our society goes, you'll only be able to see her for a couple of hours at the house since she will probably off in her 'independence' and party all night and hang out with her friends as much as possible, or keep seeing her boss for 'overtime' and not come home at all, and just keep you on the side when her friends and parties aren't going on or if she's lonely or if that hussy named Maggie at the workplace called her a slut again and needs to vent out to you.

You must consider your options careful because I don't want to hear any of this red-pill complaining coming out of your mouth any more. It's annoying, and you sound just as the women you're protesting against. You say these women are modern, but in my beliefs women have always been the same since Eve ate that apple; it's just that the attitude of women, as all things of man, is now presented in a different way. Take this advice, and do me a favor: never call me up again. Or if you're interested I can introduce you to my lady friend named Vickie Daniels, but we call her VD for short, and she can be sure to cure all your hang ups if you're well hung as long as you don't hang yourself low.

Your humble servant and friend,
Bruce Lennison

LETTER XIV

Dear Suckfist,

Why do you keep discussing me of your trauma as a little youngling? Am I a therapist for you? I have mine own troubles and need not your world's weight to bring more poundage to my shoulders. I understand we live in an age where all mouths have tongues, but that doesn't mean you can't cut yours for silence. I don't need your full testimony. At times it's best to find the beauty in light conversation, as not every being needs to be your friend after one verb, and one can enjoy the pleasures of laughter, praise, and discussion without needing to allow that pequod to sink for a conceivable whale. But because you take every conversation as the last, and took our last speech together more serious than heaven, I will now waste your time with my deepest mystery of what I felt on your discussments last night.

But the irony of your thoughts is that you have told me the story so many times I can repeat it for you within this prose within respectful measures: On a trip to some canyon out West, you and your family thought it would be best to ride horses to explore the attractions this park had to offer. However, by the unladylikeness of Fortune, there weren't any more horses and you were left as an outsider to ride the donkey, or by your perceptions a mule, named Seymour. The instructor, as you told me, benefited you the doubt by conceiving the speech that this donkey was actually better and, by his name, he would help you see more of what the park and these canyons had to offer. But you were at the tail end of these exceptions because, quoted you, Seymour the donkey liked to take his pupils close to the cliff of the mountains the peoples trailed; and because of your fear of heights and the childish belief that this Seymour would be an ass and fall off the cliff, by some stretch the fantasy gives us, you were made fearful of riding Seymour the donkey in duration of this occurrence and have been traumatized ever since.

May I remind you that this happened to you when you were eight? You are a thirty-something and should be under the American spell of what harbors a thirty-something: a career of corporate you don't like, a wife of some manners after previous divorce, two point five children, dogs, cats, a white-picket fence, kept grass from a gardener of the Mexican persuasion, baseball tickets for your sons, fresh face paint for your daughters, a minivan, a television playing Elmo, nondenominational church on Sundays, no meat on Fridays, only dance when mentions a song of praying hands like Devo, no friends except those who speak the Cowboys and are willing to play golf with you if your wife allows it, making sure your wife has each gift to her heart's desire so you can get some peaches when the air is blowing at precisely 5.25 miles per hour and the night shines a blue moon, making sure that all are your kids are in every possible extracurricular in spite of themselves, and making sure that they are in extracurriculars that but fit your liking so you can have a reason to speak of your kids with your so-called friends, make sure that you are a part of every social activity so you can be a contribute to your community, have your bills paid, and all and all making sure the portrait of your life is something Rockwell painted in a freedom of want while the inside lurks something suspicious, since the point of your American Dream is to make sure it looks to me and not yourself.

You may consider this insensitive, but I'm only relating reality that you fail to face as you're in your room, I bet, reflecting on your troubled past while watching moths die on the bulb. Or do you not even have a light because you're afraid that the attractive light will lead the flies to death from the pull? Has anyone ever told you to pop valium? If you can't grow up from this, I know not how you'll be able to face life when some old timer from Duluth accidentally runs over your pet snail or you wake one day to discover a fungus is all over your elbow. Quite frankly I hope this does happen to you so you can realize how much Nature can take her worse course as life ages.

But in all seriousness, if you happened to hear naying benouce to you in nightmares, or feel asses are following you like a private dick, then I would suggest you speak to my doctor Dr. Vinnie Boombatz; he's a gentle doctor and he's a very good doctor. How good is he? I'll put it to you this way: I called him up just last week and told him Doc, I just swallowed a bottle of sleeping pills, and he told me Have a few drinks and take a nap. Within the care of Dr. Vinnie Boombatz, he will be able to cure all of your troubles and traumas. Sometimes I see the doctor in spite of myself, but this is neither here nor there. His number is 248-434-5508, and when you speak to him tell him that Rick Astley sent you.

Remember, don't focus on anxieties of youth that stifle your entertainment. The past is the past and you must relieve yourself of that earth so you may be embraced with a new mantle opened to a brighter world and future.

Your favorite and vulnerable friend,
Kissbreech

LETTER XV

Dear Jack,

My soul was just in pangs as you were laying in that hospital bed recovering from that operation. Mine sorrow was an ocean, and had enough blues to cover the seven seas, and knew not if you'd make it or not. I was betting against it, but I'm glad just the same you are with your spirits and in recovery. But I'm writing you this letter in all seriousness, mused up by that situation in the hospital when we were transitioning you from one room to another the other day: I was carrying your luggage as well as your assortments while the nurse was guiding your bed. But while I was carrying your vetements, I'm pretty sure you were aware I was also carrying your shoes, which during the feat inhibited me from any bliss and inspired mine visage to a field of disgust as I caught a whiff of the stink embraced by the breath of your soles.

Knowing you're still in recovery, I will make light my remarks; but when I smelled your shoes, I felt as if I was slapped by Hulk Hogan and Mr. T combined in the stench. But let me not use this expression. I understand you're a science major, so I'll coin some verbatim you can understand: you people intellectualize this disease, and I guess the doctors forgot to diagnose in the hospital, as Bromhidrosis, which confounds the systems with body odor from the fear of bacteria; but we regular people intellectualize this God-forsaken disease as 'Stank Foot', or better put as 'you have some stanky ass feet.' By 'Slip, your disease compiles this colloquial: your tootsies are undifferent in likes of Jamaican sewage and can out-gas a cow from his farts from the amount of clear methane you produce by your corns. Goodness gracious, I thought I was transported to a zoo and went under a gorilla after I got a whiff of that stench! I did say I'd make this light, but how can I make light of an event that is traumatized in darkness between the depths of my mind's eye and stained for remembrance? Let me ask, have you ever gotten a bath? Have you ever considered washing yourself? What about washing your socks? Or are you a lazy mother who's hung up? Or do you purposely grow cheese between your toes? I think the doctors should have tested you for this Bromhidrosis before operating, and given you prescriptions for Right Guard or Axe before prescribing you Corticosteroids or Anticonvulsants to ease your pain, which after this letter I have to pick up for you at the CVS. But I might as well prescribe to you the Right Guard as a friendly doctor, not so you can ease the pain on yourself but so you can ease the pain you inflict upon others in spite of yourself.

I have been contemplating whether or not I should labor mine hours to see you again; I know not if it's worth it to suffocate under the fumes you brought from the underworld and endure its trials, like Aeneas in conversations with his father before discovering Rome.

I could, but I won't be versed from any Virgil to endure my name for my valiant deeds in taking on your stench, so what's the point in seeing you if mine acts will endure among the statues of futility? You may go out on me, so there's no point in being a hyperstoic for the uselessness of extremity. Why should I help you when you can't even help yourself?

You know I kid around, and all of my lines are for fun. I say all of this so you can ease the tension of yourself when you receive the letter, because I know how sensitive you get when someone brings lines of truth to your ear. But when you get out the hospital, promise me this: cure yourself of stench and become native to the scents of spring, so no trouble will be inflicted upon mine nostrils as you with your liver.

Your obedient friend,
Nanook

LETTER XVIII

Dear Makayla,

I lost my phone somewhere down the alley last night: I think I sat it down somewhere and forgot of it. I know not when I'll receive a new one but my husband says it won't take too long. You ran off last night, so I had to uber home. I assume you've eyes, a wit's end longer than a flea, an understandment of the book behind stamps, and a mind for conclusion to read this bosom of affection, as I'll but speak you to this format for the time being.

Who did you go home with? You rode with me. Regarding last night at Greenville, you told me you didn't fancy players; why's that you played a player's game by going off with Carlos, a pickup artist known to game on all these platforms, near the Skellig and made out with him in around the dark corner? Is that who you went home with? or someone else? I thought you told me you weren't going to be that hoe tonight, but instead, as you told me, you'll be a little Lucy looking for her Desi, and wanted a sweet, soft, innocent, unmasculine but passionate boy who isn't vain or carries the heart of Petruchio. By the deduction of this man type you want, we could've gone to the playground or an elementary to look at the kiddies swinging on some swings; but you insisted on being kated going to Deep Ellum and Greenville to find this worshiper of Cupid. I introduced you to my boy friend Steve, who's graduating from Tech in Bagpipping this season, who has a knack for charades, and, the most important option, the most heavenly man I know, and introduced you to Herman who's a writer and going to school in Denton, another sweetheart, but you told me Steve wasn't your type because he was only six foot two and not six foot four, and Herman was off because he was obsessed with Le Mans racing without letting you bark off about Barbie and how the actress wasn't nominated at the Oscars. None of these men you took a hit to and ruined the divine culmination Hymen could intervene. You tell me constantly how you want a man to respect you and love you for who you are, but where are you when you the shoe's on the other foot and you'll have to love the man for who he is? You say you want a Prince Charming, but how do you know you're that Snow White and Cinderella that he wants? Are you pretty, modest, proper, dress well, good at the mouth? Any man of that good fortune you so desire can pass on you as the wind blows. Why? For that art of man is rare, and women want that rare quality, and women bombard his messages as if another Oswald and Kennedy happened.

In life, you must take chances; 'tis true in art as it is in love, and I won't give ear to these Mickey Mouse visions you conceit of a false love that has no meat in its grounds. I know not how you'll find that man if you're constantly with complaints of how you're lonely and need a boyfriend, yet reject every man I introduce you to, and refuse to redownload Hinge for nicer dates. If you continue this mode of woman's fiction, and reject all the beast the approach your beauty, later in life you'll find those same men now married and find yourself all alone, with your Barbie and the discussions thereof with the mirror. It may not seem like it now, as you walk the world's beaches and extract each oyster out the clams, but soon Fortune will find thee arrogant and wheel life by your age into complete nothingness if you think you can continue this useless sleeping without affection and loneliness till you're six feet under. This isn't from thought, as many podcasts proclaim, but from experiences from woman as us who smile on Instagram, but cry when the camera's not on them; I only would to protect you from you.

I'm glad I'm married and avoided this culture of trying to sleep with as many men as if it were a badge. You've tried many times in our younger years, that are now gone with age, to convince me I'm the fool for not getting drunk off some strange syrup and not going home with each man that looks my way. Aft' some time of this life, I think I see the bells on your feet. For your style's a lonely business, and by 'Sear, I would hate to be left alone in this dating world, where women treat men as apps and delete them out their life as soon as their approached in, and where the only best men are the Casanovas looking for another nun to confirm their confused exploits, with all the other men not even given a chance and abyssed with too much paranoias to even make a second approach. I'd hate to be a man now, especially if I've to deal with woman as you who've nothing to provide for as a lover or wife, and derp around as a leaf to the wind; but let me not go off on you.

Girl, you're a genius; I know this for a fact 'cause you tell me this constantly, but if I were your mother, by 'slight, I'd smite you for thy hypocrisy and confusion. You're better than this. Anyways, don't come crying at my front door when you find out that Carlos treats you as his other shorties and keeps you for the streets, as you usually do when the player played his game on his stage takes you out the play. He knows woman like you who fall for the first man that can soliloquy, and needs not an another annoyment in his life to please him. But in all honesty, you should be on the news for your sexual conquering; for women as you always get pressed and, as Carlin once quoteth, A little brain damage isn't all that bad. Nevermind, I'm running off and making no sense hitherto. Write me back, if you're able to do so, and consider me.

Best,
Amy Jane